Selections From

Anastasia

AF621160

Alfred Music
P.O. Box 10003
Van Nuys, CA 91410-0003
alfred.com

ISBN-10: 0-7692-5393-8
ISBN-13: 978-0-7692-5393-0

Contents

From the Twentieth Century Fox Motion Picture "ANASTASIA"

A RUMOR IN ST. PETERSBURG

Lyrics by
LYNN AHRENS

Music by
STEPHEN FLAHERTY
Arranged by ROBERT SCHULTZ

gets us through the day! Hey! Have you heard? There's a ru - mor in St. Pe - ters - burg!
Have you heard what they're say - ing on the street? Al - though the Tsar did not sur - vive, one
daugh - ter may be still a - live! The Prin - cess An - a - sta - sia!
But please do not re - peat! It's a ru - mor, a leg - end, a
mys - ter - y! Some - thing's whis - pered in an al - ley - way or through a crack! It's a

1.
mp
ru - mor that's part of our his - to - ry!
They say her roy - al Grand-ma-ma will pay a roy - al sum to some-one who can bring the Prin-cess back!
We'll
cresc.
2.
find a girl to play the part and teach her what to say,
dress her up and take her to "Pa - ree!" Im - ag - ine the re - ward her dear old Grand - ma - ma will pay! Who

else could pull it off but you and me? We'll be rich! We'll be rich! We'll be
cresc.
out! We'll be out! And St. Pe-ters-burg will have some more to talk a-bout Sssh!
f
Final Chorus:
p
Have you heard? There's a ru-mor in St. Pe-ters-burg! Have you heard what they're
say-ing on the street? Hey!
f
Have you heard? There's a ru-mor in St. Pe-ters-burg!
Have you heard? Com-rades, what do you sup-pose? A fas-ci-nat-ing mys-ter-y! The
mf

Verse 2:
A ruble for this painting! It's Romanov, I swear!
Count Yusopov's pajamas! Comrades, buy the pair!
I got them from the palace. It's lined with real fur.
It could be worth a fortune if it belonged to her!

Have you heard? There's a rumor in St. Petersburg!
Have you heard what they're saying in the street?
Although the Tsar did not survive, one daughter may be still alive!
The Princess Anastasia! But please do not repeat!

It's the rumor, the legend, the mystery!
It's the Princess Anastasia who will help us fly!
You and I, friend, will go down in history!
We'll find a girl to play the part and teach her what to say,
Dress her up and take her to "Paree!"
Imagine the reward her dear old Grandmama will pay!
Who else could pull it off but you and me?
We'll be rich! We'll be rich!
We'll be out! We'll be out!
And St. Petersburg will have some more to talk about!
(To Final Chorus:)

From the Twentieth Century Fox Motion Picture "ANASTASIA"

JOURNEY TO THE PAST

Lyrics by
LYNN AHRENS

Music by
STEPHEN FLAHERTY
Arranged by ROBERT SCHULTZ

how the world can seem so vast on a jour - ney
to the past.
mf
1.
2.
Bridge:
mp
Home, love, fam - 'ly There was
once a time I must have had them too.

mf
Home, love, fam - 'ly. I will nev - er be com - plete un - til I
find you.
f
3. One step at a time. One hope, then
an - oth - er. Who knows where this road may go?
Back to who I was. On to find my fu - ture.
Things my heart still needs to know. Yes,

Verse 2:
Somewhere down this road I know someone's waiting.
Years of dreams just can't be wrong.
Arms will open wide. I'll be safe and wanted,
Finally home where I belong.
Well, starting now, I'm learning fast,
On this journey to the past.
(To Bridge:)

From the Twentieth Century Fox Motion Picture "ANASTASIA"

ONCE UPON A DECEMBER

Lyrics by
LYNN AHRENS

Music by
STEPHEN FLAHERTY
Arranged by ROBERT SCHULTZ

And a song some - one sings,
once up - on a De - cem - ber.
Some - one holds me safe and warm.
Hors - es prance through a sil - ver storm.
Fig - ures danc - ing grace - ful - ly a - cross my mem - o - ry.
mf

mf
Far a - way, long a - go,
glow - ing dim as an em - ber,
things my heart used to know,
things it yearns to re - mem - ber.
rit.

A little slower
p
And a song some - one sings,
once up - on a De - cem -
poco rit.
ber.
a tempo
pp

From the Twentieth Century Fox Motion Picture "ANASTASIA"

LEARN TO DO IT

Lyrics by
LYNN AHRENS

Music by
STEPHEN FLAHERTY
Arranged by ROBERT SCHULTZ

Was I wild? Wrote the book! But you'd be - have when your fa - ther gave that look! I -
mf
mag-ine how it was! Your long for-got-ten past! We've lots and lots to teach you and the
time is go - ing fast!
f
1. Now,
mp
Verse:
shoul-ders back and stand up tall. And do not walk, but try to float. I
feel a lit - tle fool - ish. Am I float - ing? Like a lit - tle boat! You

give a bow. What hap - pens now? Your
hand re - ceives a kiss!
Chorus:
Most of all, re - mem - ber this: If
cresc.
f
I can learn to do it,
you can learn to do it.
Some - thing in you knows it. There's
noth - ing to it!
Fol - low in my foot-steps,
shoe by shoe!
You can learn to do it
1.
too!
2. Now,
mp
2.
too!

mp
Next, we memorize the names of the royalty.
Now, here we have Kro - pot - kin. Shot Po - tem - kin. In the bot - kin.
Oh! And dear old Un - cle Van - ya loved his vod - ka. Got it, An - ya?
No! The Bar - on Push - kin, he was short! Count An - a - to - ly had a
wart! Count Ser - gei wore a feath - ered hat! I hear he's got - ten ver - y

fat! And I re - call his yel - low cat.
I don't believe we told her that.
Chorus:
1. If
you can learn to do it, I can learn to do it!
Don't know how you knew it. I sim - ply knew it!
Sud - den - ly I feel like some - one new!
An - ya, you're a dream come true!
2. If

Verse 2:
Now, elbows in and sit up straight.
And never slurp the stroganoff.
I never cared for stroganoff.
She said that like a Romanov!
The samovar. The caviar. Desert and then goodnight!
Not until you get this right!

Chorus 2:
If I can learn to do it, you can learn to do it.
Pull yourself together and you'll pull through it!
Tell yourself it's easy and it's true!
You can learn to do it too!
(to 2nd ending)

Final Chorus:
If I can learn to do it, you can learn to do it!
Pull yourself together and you'll pull through it!
Tell yourself it's easy and it's true!
You can learn to do it!
Nothing to it!
You can learn to do it too!

From the Twentieth Century Fox Animated Motion Picture "ANASTASIA"

PARIS HOLDS THE KEY (TO YOUR HEART)

Words and Music by
LYNN AHRENS and STEPHEN FLAHERTY
Arranged by ROBERT SCHULTZ

heart, and all of Par - is plays a part. Just
stroll two by two down what we call "La Rue," and soon all Par -
is will be sing - ing to you! Par - is holds the key to L'a -
mour, and not e - ven Freud knows the cure!
To Coda
There's love in the air! At the Fol - lies Ber - gere! The

French have it down to an art! Par - is holds the
key to your heart!
non legato
mp
When you're feel - ing blue come to Le
Mou - lin.
When your heart says, "Don't" the French say, "Do!"
When you think you can't, you'll find you can - can!
D.S. 𝄋 al Coda
Ev-ery-one can can - can! You can can - can too!
2. Par -
poco cresc.
mf

Verse 2:
Paris holds the key to her past,
Yes, Princess, I've found you at last.
No more pretend. You'll be gone. That's the end...

Paris holds the key to your heart!
You'll be très jolie and so smart!
Come dance through the night and forget all your woes!
The city of light! Where a rose is a rose!
And one never knows what will start!
Paris holds the key to her heart!

From the Twentieth Century Fox Animated Motion Picture "ANASTASIA"

IN THE DARK OF THE NIGHT

Lyrics by
LYNN AHRENS

Music by
STEPHEN FLAHERTY
Arranged by ROBERT SCHULTZ

Then I o-pened my eyes and the night-mare was me!
I was once the most mys - ti - cal man in all Rus - sia.
When the roy - als be-trayed me, they made a mis - take!
My curse made each of them pay,
but one lit - tle girl got a - way!
Lit - tle An - ya, be - ware, Ras-pu-tin's a - wake!

Chorus:
In the dark of the night, e - vil will find her!
In the dark of the night, just be - fore dawn. Re -
venge will be sweet when the curse is com-plete!
In the dark of the night, she'll be gone!
dim.
through!

In the dark of the night, e - vil will find her.
In the dark of the night, ter - ror comes true! My
dear, here's a sign, it's the end of the line!
In the dark of the night!
In the dark of the night!
mp
Come, my min - ions! Rise for your mas - ter! Let your e - vil

Verse 2:
I can feel that my powers are slowly returning.
Tie my sash and a dash of cologne for that smell.
As the pieces fall into place,
I'll see her crawl into place.
Dasvidanya, Anya, your grace, farewell!

Chorus 2:
In the dark of the night, terror will strike her!
In the dark of the night, evil will brew!
Soon she will feel that her nightmares are real!
In the dark of the night, she'll be through!
(To 2nd ending)